ROCHESTER

Today there are fifteen Rochesters in the United States and many others throughout the world, which owe the origin of their name to the "mother" of all Rochesters: Rochester, County of Kent, England.

The original Rochester can trace its history to 51 B.C., or the Roman occupation of the British Isles. Today, Rochester, England, is a community whose size is nearly one-third that of Rochester, Minnesota. It is located 26 miles southeast of London on the right bank of the Medway. It is also situated on the main highway from London to Canterbury and thence to Dover. As such, it was in the path of all invading armies that followed Caesar's Legions and ended with the Norman Conquest in 1066.

After the Romans, the Saxons occupied it for about 600 years. Most of English royalty have visited it. Charles Dickens lived in Rochester, England, from 1856 until the time of his death in 1870. Its earliest charter was granted by Richard I in 1189. The Rochester Cathedral and Castle, built during Norman times, are still standing.

Needless to say, Rochester has a rich history.

Edited remarks made by Rochester Rotary Club historian
E.H. Schlitgus, on May 25, 1961, as part of the club's 36th anniversary.
(Courtesy of Olmsted County Historical Society)

Credits:

Photography: Dean Riggott

Foreword: Dr. Paul Scanlon

Captions: Mike Dougherty & Dean Riggott

History: Mike Dougherty

Design & Layout: Dean Riggott

Editing: Randi Kallas, Mike Dougherty & Dr. Paul Scanlon

First edition / Soft cover / $ 24.95

Library of Congress Card Number: 2003092846
ISBN # 0-9659875-3-1

Produced and published in the United States of America
by Dean Riggott Photography - Copyright © 2003

Printed in the Republic of Korea by Doosan Printing

Dean Riggott Photography
831 10 1/2 Street SW
Rochester, MN 55902
Phone: 507-285-5076

www.riggottphoto.com
riggottphoto@charter.net

ROCHESTER

MINNESOTA

A Visual and Historic Journey

Photography
DEAN RIGGOTT

Text
MIKE DOUGHERTY

DEAN RIGGOTT PHOTOGRAPHY
ROCHESTER, MINNESOTA

Acknowledgments:

I would like to thank the following people for their help, support and cooperation:

My father, Don Riggott, who inspired me to become a photographer and has offered support and guidance throughout my life.

Dr. Paul Scanlon, who shared his vast knowledge of Rochester's history and wrote the foreword of this book.

Mike Dougherty, John Hunziker and Randi Kallas, who helped research, write and edit this book.

And my wife, Kati, whose love, support and encouragement carried me along in this project.

Foreword

by Dr. Paul Scanlon

"I was born right here." – Randy Newman lyric

In the summer of 1978, I was living in Baltimore, having just moved from Rochester, permanently (I thought), for the second time. As I rode a shuttle bus, I overheard a conversation about Rochester, Minnesota. Why would anyone in Baltimore be interested in Rochester? As locals will recall, the great summer flood of 1978 had captured a brief moment of national attention for Rochester. Having grown up here, I reveled in the moment of attention for my hometown, even as I worried about it, needing detail not available in the national news. The flood is now part of Rochester's history, and a very important factor in the evolution of the city over the past 25 years.

The Zumbro River provided some of the most memorable experiences of my youth, playing in and near the river. As I reached my teen years, canoeing and camping on the Zumbro became an annual ritual, floating and paddling to Lake Zumbro or Zumbro Falls, occasionally all the way to the confluence with the Mississippi at Kellogg. The Zumbro is not the best canoeing river in the world – full of obstructions – fallen trees, rocks, rapids. (Not a bad metaphor for life: moving along despite all that.) The Zumbro has been a central element in the history of Rochester, both literally and figuratively.

When I was a kid, I thought Rochester had no history. We were just a small town of no particular interest except, perhaps, for the large clinic that employed my father. Rochester has, since I was a kid, and perhaps before, been renowned among its youth for the fact that there is nothing to do. Many of my affluent friends enjoyed the luxury of a summer home on a lake, or at the very least, a boat on the Mississippi. I felt unfortunate not to have that luxury. Living in a county with no natural lake, in the Land of 10,000 Lakes, we don't fit the image of what a small Minnesota town ought to be. When I was an undergraduate at the University of Minnesota, a friend, who was a native of the eastern United States, interviewed for admission to Mayo Medical School. When he returned, he cynically commented that Rochester was like an eastern ocean resort town, but without the ocean. I had no response and little insight into the uniqueness or the history of my hometown.

I returned to Rochester in 1984, after finishing my training in pulmonary and critical care medicine, to begin working at Mayo Clinic. I had many misgivings.

Thomas Wolfe wrote: "You can't go home again," but here I was. Rochester had changed somewhat. It was larger; there were new developments, and most of my old friends were gone. I was struck, however, by the many ways in which it was the same. Daniel Pinkwater parodied Wolfe by writing: "It's not that you can't go home again. It's that most people know better." I struggled with that. As a child, it is easy to blame one's parents for having to live in a town that one does not appreciate. As an adult, I needed to justify my decision to return here, not only to myself, but to my wife and children. I loved my work and I believed the assertion that Rochester is a good home for young families. But is it just a sleepy little town with little to offer other than employment and safety?

I learned more about the city, both the "new" and the "old" Rochester. I found that one could learn more by seeing the modern reflected in the artifacts of history and by learning the city in four dimensions, including time as it relates to place. Place is defined by its three dimensions, but equally by the fourth dimension, time – by history. Like an old friend or family member, familiarity breeds not contempt, but a deeper appreciation of the subtleties of the subject of study. As I learned more about the city and its history, I became more bonded to it, and began to feel more a part of it.

History is fun. One of the most frequently asked questions among visitors to Rochester is, "Why in the world did they build the Mayo Clinic here in the middle of the cornfields?" The answer predates the Mayo brothers and includes malaria, political intrigues, scandals in the religious orders, an Indian uprising, the Civil War, and not one but two tornadoes.

Midwesterners often feel like historical neophytes compared with natives of eastern states or Europe. However, the history of American medicine is a recent history. Saint Marys Hospital opened in 1889, the same year as Johns Hopkins Hospital. The evolution of American medicine and its emergence as the leader in the world of medicine occurred during the careers of the Mayo brothers. Rochester was right in the middle of that history.

What were the Mayo brothers like? Peas in a pod? Identical personalities? Not even close! They were as different as their homes. Charlie was a character – a farmer, a hunter, an automobile enthusiast, and a hale-fellow-well-met. His home, Mayowood, is a big, rambling informal house several miles out of town whose enormous estate was once filled with gardens, stables, a dairy, several working farms, and a man-made lake with 50 islands and a Venetian gondola. Will, by contrast, was an austere gentleman.

His home, now the Mayo Foundation House, is much more formal – beautiful and comfortable, but not cozy. Professionally, Charlie was the brilliant surgeon, but was far less interested in administration than his brother. He was loved by those who knew him. Will was more serious, somewhat distant and formal. Will was the administrator. He was an excellent surgeon, but developed his surgical expertise in areas where Charlie was least interested.

Many other questions piqued my interest in Rochester. For example: What happened to the local Indians and why do you hear so little about them? What were the origins of the names Rochester, Olmsted, Zumbro and Bear Creek? Why is Rochester called the Queen City? How did citizens of Rochester participate in the political and military history of our country? Who are Rochester's four Nobel laureates? What happened to the Schuster Brewery, the Queen City Mill, the old firehall, and the marble statues of Lincoln and Washington? Who was Harold Crawford? How did the Mayo Clinic evolve and who were the key players? Where did all these parks come from? Where were College and Zumbro streets? How did other industries, such as agriculture, inn-keeping, retail trade and technology evolve with the clinic, local government entities and the growing population?

Knowledge of history provides an understanding of this place. Another requirement for learning to appreciate Rochester is an appreciation of the subtle beauty of the northern prairie – the monochromatic vistas of winter, the soft rolling hills of the prairie, the small scale of natural features. This part of the country lacks the grandeur of the western United States – the mountains particularly. The magnitude of western beauty is not here. Instead, we have a smaller, subtler beauty, sometimes only appreciated after adapting to severe cold or other conditions that can be distracting, to say the least.

I eventually resolved most of my uncertainty about living in Rochester by learning to appreciate its small-scale beauty, enjoying the advantages of small distances, knowing more about it, and becoming an active participant in the life of the city. I live downtown now, right on the river. I enjoy being immersed in the city and watching it and the river both move and change with the seasons.

Dean Riggott is also a native of Rochester. His photography captures our local beauty with crystal-clear images and vivid colors we find often in our dreams, but only on a good day in reality. Rochester is fortunate to have a photographer of his caliber to fortify our belief in the beauty of this city. The subtle beauty of our hometown can be difficult to bring to mind on a dreary day. Riggott's photography does just that. His first book, *Rochester: The Images*, was very popular with both residents and visitors. It presented a composite that said: "This is Rochester – it is a beautiful place if you look carefully." His new book, *Rochester, Minnesota: A Visual and Historic Journey*, supplements the images of his previous work and adds the historical dimension that long-term residents, new members of the community, and visitors can all appreciate.

Beyond simple enjoyment, an appreciation for that which is beautiful or historically significant in our community will promote preservation for future generations. By understanding and preserving what we have, we build our history for our children. Rochester has mourned the loss of many of our historical buildings including the 1914 redbrick Mayo Clinic building, the original homes of the Mayo brothers, the Soldier's Field bathhouse, and most of the original downtown churches, hotels and commercial buildings. Conversely, we have recognized and sought to preserve treasures such as the Plummer Building, the Foundation House, the Chateau Theater, the Calvary Episcopal Church, the Chicago & Great Western Railroad station, the Healy Chapel, the E. Starr Judd home, the Frank Lloyd Wright homes, the "Stone Barn," The Broadstreet Café, the Wonder Bread factory and much of "Pill Hill."

Other landmarks teeter in the uncertainty of inadequate funding or uncertain ownership, including Mayowood, the Plummer House, the remaining original downtown hotels and commercial buildings including the BF Goodrich store and the original Telephone Building, the Second Street Victorian houses, the ear-of-corn water tower, Folwell School, the Avalon Hotel, and the sandstone hills on the northeast edges of the city. A greater appreciation of the beauty and value of what we have will help us to identify what we wish to save for future generations. This volume is a useful guide in that endeavor.

– Rochester native Dr. Paul Scanlon is Director of the Pulmonary Clinical Research Center and Pulmonary Function Lab and Chair of Humanities in Medicine at Mayo Clinic in Rochester. He is also a former member and former president of the Rochester School Board and a former member of the Rochester Art Center Board. Paul lives with his wife, Maggie, and has two adult children.

Chardonnay Cuisine Exceptionnelle

Chardonnay Cuisine Exceptionnelle has specialized in New French cuisine since it was opened by Mark Weimer and Lisa Michel in 1991. With an extensive selection of French, American and Spanish wines in its cellar, *Wine Spectator* magazine has consistently ranked it among 300 of the world's top restaurants. Before the restaurant's birth, the 1890 Victorian house was a bed and breakfast called Canterbury Inn. The Broadstreet Cafe was started here before moving to its location at First Avenue Northeast in 1986.

Saint Marys Chapel

This Italian Renaissance-style chapel was built in 1904 at the east end of Saint Marys Hospital and expanded in 1930 to accommodate the crowds that came for Sunday Mass. The chapel features an altar of ivory-colored Carrara marble, a canopy of red velvet and a statue of the Virgin Mary holding the infant Jesus at the center of the altar. Its 16 pillars are unpolished pearl white granite from Cold Spring, Minn.

"Constellation Earth"

"Constellation Earth," a bronze cast sculpture by Minnesota artist Paul T. Granlund, serves as the centerpiece of a quiet corner park on the east side of Rochester Methodist Hospital's Eisenberg Building. The seven dancing figures symbolize the Earth's seven continents and the interdependence of human beings. Their hands and feet touch in a gesture of peace and unity as their bodies stretch into space to form an open sphere.

Bluebells

The beauty of a trip along Rochester's bicycle and walking trails can be found all around. It depends on what season, too. Here, a blanket of blue-bells covers the wooded ground near the Zumbro River on the trail that leads to Mayowood in southwest Rochester. Many colorful varieties of wild flowers can be found pushing upward in spring on the hillsides and in the tree-shaded valleys. In fall, the wooded trails come alive as the leaves begin to change colors.

'Tis the Season

A moonlit December night can seem magical in downtown Rochester with holiday lights twinkling in boulevard trees and outlining the skyways. The Rochester Park & Recreation Department has decorated Rochester's central business district with holiday lights, garlands and wreaths since 1989. The decorating process begins in November and it takes about three weeks to string 22,000 lights that stretch 33,000 feet.

Plummer House

The genius of Dr. Henry Plummer was showcased not only in the Plummer Building, but also in the home he built with his wife, Daisy. The 49-room English Tudor mansion, completed in 1924, included some unusual features for homes of that era: an intercom, a central vacuum-cleaning system and the first gas furnace in Rochester. The Plummer House is now owned by the City of Rochester and maintained by the Park & Recreation Department.

Apple Orchard

A deer pauses during its evening dinner in the Assisi Heights orchard. In 1949, the Franciscan sisters purchased the property from Dr. L.B. Wilson on what was then known as "Walnut Hill" northwest of Rochester. Dr. Wilson first planted the 20-acre orchard in 1924 and harvested 1,300 apple trees. Currently, the sisters grow six varieties on 97 trees spread over two acres. There were 180 bushels harvested in 2002.

Veterans Memorial

The Soldiers Field Veterans Memorial honors those from southeast Minnesota who served the nation. Volunteers raised money for the memorial, valued at $3.5 million to $5 million. The memorial includes the Wall of Remembrance with the names of 2,000 veterans from southeast Minnesota who lost their lives, the Walk of Remembrance with the names of more than 4,000 veterans and 50 trees to represent the 50 states.

Plummer Carillon

The Plummer Building was opened in 1928 with its distinctive four-story carillon tower. The bell tower was conceived by Dr. Will Mayo after he became fascinated with the bells on a trip to Belgium. The 23 bells installed in the tower came from a foundry in England and were dedicated by the Mayo brothers to the American soldier. Thirty-three more bells were added in 1977. Weekly lunchtime and evening concerts fill the air in downtown Rochester.

Silver Lake Path

A canopy of maple trees sprinkles the orange and red leaves of autumn on the bike path along the northeast side of Silver Lake. The city of Rochester maintains 77 parks covering more than 2,800 acres, including 38 miles of walking and biking trails and 63 playgrounds. Recreation enthusiasts can travel by paved trails to all quadrants of the city on routes that take them through neighborhoods, parks and downtown Rochester.

City Market

Foundation House

J.P. Zubay & Co. City Market is one of Rochester's premiere delicatessens. The deli is in a restored downtown building that once housed the Rochester Commercial Club, which later became the Chamber of Commerce. The City Market specializes in New York-style deli sandwiches, soups, salads and pastas. It also features selected food items from the Broadstreet Cafe, City Cafe, Newt's and The Redwood Room, all of which are owned and operated by Creative Cuisine Company.

After Dr. Charlie Mayo built his home, Mayowood, Dr. William Mayo built a Tudor-style house with a Kasota stone exterior in 1918. Built on Fourth Street Southwest, the tower in front housed Dr. Will's office. In 1938, the house was donated to the Mayo Foundation. Known today as Mayo Foundation House, the home is the setting for special events and Mayo educational functions.

River Bend

Bright red Euonymus Alatus accents the bike path and bridge over Silver Creek where it spills into the Zumbro River south of Silver Lake. Warm, sunny days turn the paths into bustling highways of walkers, runners, in-line skaters and bicyclists. The city's 38 miles of paved trails edge along many of Rochester's parks and playgrounds and provide routes for travel and exercise through downtown and out to each of the city's quadrants.

First Avenue

An early-evening stroll along First Avenue Southwest in downtown Rochester is a common activity for visitors and diners during the spring and summer months. Here, in front of old City Hall, pedestrians can stop to admire the architecture and the art deco lights that mark the front door to what is now an apartment complex. It's worth walking a few blocks to admire and inspect the downtown's architecture, which mixes the old with the new.

Chihuly Sculptures

Intricate bulbs and twists adorn the blown-glass sculpture pieces hanging in the Mayo Nurses Atrium of the Gonda Building. The creation of artist Dale Chihuly is made up of 1,375 pieces of glass and consists of 13 chandeliers ranging in size from 225 pounds and 4 feet in diameter to 1,225 pounds and 10 feet in diameter, a total of 6,000 pounds. The sculptures are among the many art pieces in Mayo Clinic's newest building.

Seneca Foods

South of downtown Rochester's distinctive skyline is another landmark structure: Seneca Foods' ear of corn water tower. The water tower, which often makes the list in travel books for quirky landmarks, was built in 1931. The 150-foot tall water tower holds 50,000 gallons and is capable of pumping more than 1,000 gallons of water a minute. Between 750,000 to 1 million gallons of water are used daily during the busy summer vegetable canning season.

Old Chateau Theatre

The Chateau Dodge Theatre opened in 1927 on the site of the former Dodge Lumber Company. The first movie shown there featured Joan Crawford in "Spring Fever." Balconies and turrets decorated the front and sides of the 1,497-seat theater, which cost $400,000 to build. In 1983, the theater closed and sat boarded up and vacant for 10 years before being renovated and turned into a unique bookstore by Barnes & Noble Bookstores in 1994.

Gonda Building

The Leslie and Susan Gonda Building, Mayo Clinic's newest building, altered the city's distinctive skyline when it opened in October 2001. The total cost of the project was $375 million, nearly half of which was given or pledged by Mayo Clinic benefactors. The building added more than 1.5 million square feet to the downtown campus and connects to the Charlton Building to the north and the Mayo Building to the south.

Snowy Spruce

A heavy snow laces the spruce trees of East Park with a white accent on a February morning. The park on the city's east side is the entryway to the former Rochester State Hospital campus. The state hospital was in operation from 1879 to 1982, but was eventually closed and sold in parts to other government agencies. The 1,400-acre campus is a mix of buildings and park land that encompasses a wide range of terrain, flora and fauna.

Night Lights

While the skyline of Rochester has changed through the decades, it has maintained two constants: the lighted Plummer Building and the red neon Kahler Hotel sign, shown here before Mayo Clinic's Gonda Building went up. Mayo Clinic's expansion has put the skyline in a constant state of change. The growth has further established Mayo Clinic's reputation throughout the world. As a community, Rochester's reputation has grown beyond its borders, too, gaining worldwide attention with various magazines ranking it as one of the nation's most livable cities.

John Kruesel's

A kerosene lamp sparked John Kruesel's interest in antiques when he was just 8. "I was fascinated with it and after that I started acquiring historical objects and knowledge," says Kruesel, who has operated his antique store on Rochester's Historic Third Street since 1975. The building was erected in 1874 and has been home to an implement dealership, a coal and wood-fired stove business, a sign company, a sewing center and a hobby shop.

Sekapp Orchard

Ken and Joyce Kappauf have operated Sekapp Orchard for more than 40 years. Today, they operate it with their son, Fred. The Kappaufs bought the orchard from Ben Dunn, a local school teacher, in 1962. The land has been an orchard since World War I. In season, Sekapp offers 30 varieties of apples, strawberries, raspberries, fresh garden produce, pumpkins, fall decorations, jams, maple syrup and honey. Their seasons begin in June and end in December.

River Crossing

A pedestrian bridge links walkers and bikers to the north side of the Zumbro River in southwest Rochester. This stretch of trail near Bamber Valley Road winds its way to Mayowood Lake near Mayowood Mansion. The city of Rochester maintains more than 38 miles of paved trails that stretch to each quadrant of the city, linking many of the city's 77 parks. Large portions of the trail follow the Zumbro River and several of its tributaries.

Quarry Hill

Quarry Hill, on Rochester's east side, includes a nature learning center, 290 acres of park land and five miles of walking and skiing trails. Originally part of the State Hospital farm, Quarry Hill was purchased by the city in 1965 and includes a fishing pond, sandstone caves, a limestone quarry and a restored oak savanna. A paved path links the park to downtown and the city's trail system.

City Hall Atrium

City offices ring the three floors around the rotunda of City Hall. The dome, painted cream, blue and gold, is capped with a skylight 65 feet overhead. Hallways with wood-trimmed railings and balconies encircle the second and third floors. City Hall is connected to the Olmsted County Government Center and was funded by a special half-cent sales tax levied on merchandise sold in Rochester. The project cost $11 million and was completed in 1996.

Bronzed Brothers

The bronze Mayo brothers sculpture at the entrance of Mayo Civic Center pierces the fog on a winter evening. The sculpture was commissioned by the Mayo Memorial Association Inc., and dedicated in 1952. The sculpture was among the last major works by the late James Earle Fraser, a Winona native. It was part of a memorial mall on the south side of Mayo Civic Center before it was moved to its current site in the late 1980s.

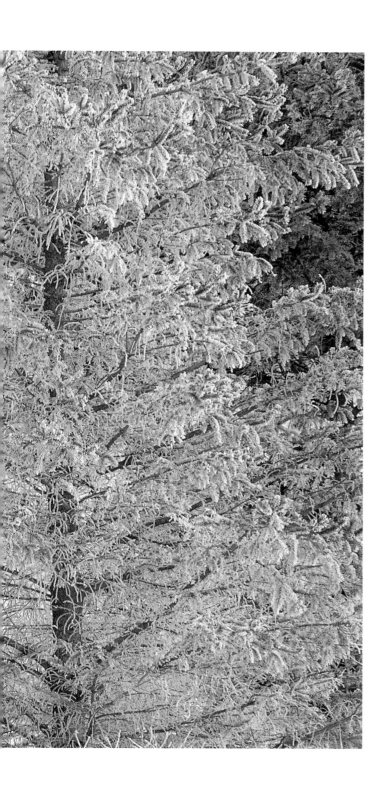

Sitting Idle

A 1020 McCormick-Deering tractor, circa 1936, sits alone in a snowy field on the Chuck Passe farm near Rochester. Passe, who works construction and farms part time, said the tractor hasn't been used since the late 1980s when it was in a shop fire. The small farm has been in Passe's family since 1949. Farms in the area produce annual harvests of corn, soybeans, alfalfa and a variety of fruits and vegetables.

Pill Hill

"Pill Hill" is considered one of the city's most distinguished neighborhoods, noted for the quantity of architecturally significant houses and its historic association with the medical professionals who reside there. The area is a residential historic district on the National Register of Historical Places. Homes in this neighborhood were built from the late 1890s to 1930. This Queen Ann style home at 716 Fourth St. S.W. was built in 1895 by a Rochester pharmacist.

Central Park

The 12-foot, three-tiered cast iron fountain in Central Park, Rochester's oldest city park, creates a peaceful view and sound on the northern edge of downtown. The land was donated by William D. Lowry and platted in 1856. The park's first fountain was added in 1887 and remained until it was dismantled in the 1930s. The current fountain was installed in 1976, but was removed for repairs after it was struck by an automobile in 1997.

City Cafe

City Cafe opened in 2003 after a successful 20-year run as Henry Wellington. In the 1930s, owner Newt Holland operated it as a grocery market. In the 1950s, he added a second floor to the building, Holland's Cafeteria & Bakery. It closed in 1977 and was re-opened by Creative Cuisine in 1978 as The Bank Restaurant. In 1980, Newt's was opened upstairs, named in honor of Newt Holland. The Bank closed in 1983 when it was remodeled into Henry Wellington.

Plummer Doors

Flour City Ornamental Iron Company of Minneapolis crafted the Plummer Building's 16-foot tall bronze doors with design squares to symbolize education, domestic arts, mechanical arts, fine arts, science and agriculture. The 5 1/2 -inch thick doors each weigh 2 tons and are only closed to mark a great loss to Mayo or the nation, such as when the Mayo brothers died in 1939, President Kennedy's assassination in 1963 and after the Sept. 11, 2001, terrorist attacks on New York City and Washington, D.C.

49

Oak Savanna

The first settlers in Olmsted County found prairie land with grasses that stood taller than a man. In 1998, a 20-acre hilltop within Quarry Hill Park was restored to an oak savanna. Native plants and grasses were planted in the area, which already contained a sizeable number of burr and red oaks. The savanna's plants, grasses, wildflowers and trees serve as habitat for many birds, mammals and insects.

The Broadstreet

The Broadstreet is one of Rochester's favorite fine dining spots. Housed in the R.C. Drips & Co. Grocer Warehouse, its interior is a mixture of exposed brick and hardwood floors. As a warehouse, it once supplied area grocery stores via the railroad, whose tracks still run past the building. The restaurant specializes in European, Mediterranean and American cuisine, and has been here since 1986, after moving from the Victorian house that is now Chardonnay Cuisine Exceptionnelle on Second Street Southwest.

Sunset at Silver Lake

Bathed in the evening light and steam from Silver Lake, a gaggle of geese stay warm in the water with their beaks nestled under a wing. Even on sub-zero days, the geese find warmth in the discharge water from Rochester Public Utilities' coal-fired Silver Lake Power Plant. The plant began operation in 1948 and the flock on the lake doubled in size the following winter and continued to increase thereafter. Today, a flock of about 4,000 calls the lake home year-round.

Saint Marys

Saint Marys Hospital was established in 1889 by the Sisters of St. Francis and run by Dr. W.W. Mayo and his physician sons, Will and Charlie. It was the first general hospital in southeastern Minnesota and the first in a series of medical institutions that today make up Mayo Medical Center. Mayo Eugenio Litta Children's Hospital, an 85-bed hospital within Saint Marys, serves pediatric patients. The hospital has undergone almost regular expansion since it was first constructed.

Calvary Episcopal

Calvary Episcopal Church is the oldest church building in Rochester. It was established as a parish in 1860 and a small chapel was built in 1863. The church, which was consecrated in 1866 in the center of town on land donated by city founder George Head, has several Tiffany stained-glass windows. More buildings have been added, including the parish hall designed by Rochester architect Harold Crawford. Its shaded courtyard is the setting for outdoor concerts in the summer.

Stoppel Farm

The George Stoppel farmhouse has withstood the tests of time and now anchors part of the Olmsted County History Center. Stoppel immigrated from Germany in 1849 and eventually traveled to Rochester by oxcart in 1856. Stones for the house were quarried from a nearby hillside. An equally rugged barn was built near the house. Stoppel planted subsistence crops first, followed by potatoes, hay and corn. The 1880 Agricultural Census listed the total area of the Stoppel Farm at 150 acres.

Flying High

The Wells Fargo balloon is a common sight in the Rochester sky with Dr. Clay Cowl captaining it on calm, quiet mornings and early evenings. As many as three people can ride in it, while a three- to four-person ground crew tracks it from below. Inflated, it is as tall as a seven-story building and weighs more than 2,600 pounds. It can fly for 1 1/2 hours in the summer and 2 1/2 hours in the winter.

Rural Farmstead

Crimson sumac leaves of early fall
frame the Harold R. Nelson farm in
the rolling hills along Olmsted County
Road 1, south of Rochester. Harold
and his wife, Eleanor, started farming
in 1963. Their sons, Mark and
Raymond, now rent the farm from
their parents, maintaining the family's
touch with the land. While health care
contributes greatly to the county's
economic picture, agriculture and
agribusiness quietly account for one-
third of the jobs in Olmsted County.

Mayowood Barns

When Dr. Charles H. Mayo established
the Mayowood Dairy Farm, mules
delivered milk to 38 customers. In
1925, the Supremacy Dairy joined
forces with the Mayowood Dairy
Farm to form the Rochester Dairy Co.
The barns were retained by Mayowood
Enterprises in 1965 when the Mayo
family mansion and a small portion of
land was turned over to the Olmsted
County Historical Society. The remaining buildings are on the National
Register of Historic Places.

Morning Swim

Three goslings swim between the
protective cover of their parents in a
quiet inlet of Silver Lake. At the end
of the 19th century, over-hunting
reduced Canada goose populations to
near extinction. Dr. Charles H. Mayo
started a flock at his farm with a pair
in the early 1920s. In 1962, it was
discovered that the Silver Lake flock
was made up primarily of giant
Canada geese, which had been
presumed extinct.

Peace Fountain

Rochester resident and international-
ly known sculptor Charles Eugene
Gagnon was commissioned by the
City of Rochester to create the Peace
Fountain. The bronze sculpture is 12
feet high and weighs 3,700 pounds.
It was dedicated in 1989 in the
downtown Peace Plaza. The 57
peace doves symbolize the 50 states
and seven continents and the human
spirit's unending quest for peace.

Blue Moon

A "blue moon" rises over the Mayo, Hilton and Guggenheim buildings of Mayo Clinic's downtown Rochester complex as the setting sun reflects off the buildings. A blue moon refers to the second full moon in a single calendar month. The final blue moon of the 20th century occurred on May 22, 1997. The Mayo Building was completed in 1955, although at the time it was only 12 stories high. By 1969, it was expanded to 21 floors.

University Atrium

The University Center Rochester atrium greets students at this unique higher education facility. Rochester Community and Technical College, the University of Minnesota and Winona State University are all housed at UCR. Students take courses in programs from certificate through graduate levels in business, education, health sciences, technology and liberal arts. The sculpture in the atrium cost $102,000 when it was installed in 1993. Its 84 strips of glass capture and bend light at all times of day.

Aquarius Club

Dooley's Lounge and Grill was turned into the Aquarius Club in 1989 when Tom Murphy and Mick Kane renovated the popular southeast Rochester night spot into a club with a futuristic dance floor. A new laser light show was installed in 1993. Five colors of laser beams are projected from a booth above the dance floor and bounced at angles via 50 mirrors. The operator uses a computer program to direct the beams in unison with the music.

Memorial Parkway

The sweet smell of apple blossoms fills Memorial Parkway in south-west Rochester shortly before the trees shed their pink blossom petals. Memorial Parkway is known for its abundance of American Colonial-style homes, many of which were designed and lived in by Francis H. Underwood. It also is a picturesque approach to Soldiers Field, a sprawling park that includes a unique memorial to the region's veterans, a golf course, swimming pool, tennis courts, running track and softball fields.

Kelly's Orchard

The windmill that stands tall at
Kelly's Orchard north of Rochester
was moved to the site from a farm
in the Whitewater area in 1965.
Kelly's Orchard was opened nine
years before the windmill's arrival
by Paul Kelly, a junior and senior
high school biology teacher in
Rochester. The orchard once con-
sisted of more than 1,500 trees. The
orchard is now operated by Paul's
son, Kevin, and his wife, Cheryl.

Gonda Building

The construction of Mayo's 20-story Gonda Building began in 1998 and a limited number of floors were opened in October 2001. It took several years to move medical personnel and equipment into the building floor-by-floor. The building, which could be expanded to 30 floors, integrates patient care, research and education activities. It contains examination, procedure and operating rooms, as well as areas for educational events and clinical research.

Old City Hall

Once the hub of government activity, Rochester's old City Hall is now home to 22 upscale apartments. The $1.9 million project in 1998 turned the mayor's office into a living room with a fireplace and the judge's bench from the council chambers into the centerpiece of a lofted bedroom. The art deco building, with its highly decorated ceilings, silver-plated light fixtures and terrazo floors, replaced the original city hall in 1932.

Historic Third Street

Just off busy Broadway is Historic Third Street. Visitors will find an outdoor table at Daube's Konditorei & German Restaurant. The German-inspired restaurant's facade is from the original M.C. Lawler's Cleaners, an art deco building designed by Harold Crawford, which once stood at Broadway and Center Street. Historic Third Street is a one-block stretch of buildings that now house restaurants, a jewelry store and antique shops.

Rochester Skyline

Rochester's skyline, captured prior to the construction of the Gonda Building, shows a city that has seen steady growth through the decades. Rochester became Minnesota's third-largest city in 2002, when state officials estimated the city's population at 89,325, surpassing Duluth and trailing only Minneapolis and St. Paul. A majority of the growth is attributed to the strong, steady expansion of Mayo Clinic, one of the world's premier medical centers.

Assisi Heights

Situated on 100 acres atop one of
the highest hills in Olmsted County,
Assisi Heights is the motherhouse of
the Sisters of St. Francis. Mother
Mary Alfred Moes, founder of the
order, convinced her friend, Dr.
W.W. Mayo, that Rochester needed
a general hospital, and together they
established Saint Marys Hospital in
1889. Assisi Heights was built from
1952 to 1955 to resemble the
Franciscan convent in Assisi, Italy,
home of the nuns' patron saint.

Old Farmall

The last of the evening sunlight
settles on an F-14 Farmall tractor at
the Allen and Jennifer Whipple home
north of Rochester. The tractor,
which was likely built during the
Great Depression, was the first tractor Allen bought in 1950 with money
he earned working part time at
Libby's Foods in Rochester. "It's
sentimental," said Allen, who grew
up the youngest of 12 children on a
farm in Zumbro Falls, Wabasha
County.

Resting Place

The Mayo family gravesite at Oakwood Cemetery in northeast Rochester is captured at early evening a few days after Memorial Day in 2003. From left to right are the graves of Hattie Damon, William J., Louise A., William W., Phoebe L., Charles H., Edith Graham and Dorothy Mayo. The headstones of Dr. Will, left, and Dr. Charlie, are marked with American flags and bronze veteran's markers for their service during World War I.

Heritage House

Sitting at the northeast corner of Central Park, Heritage House is an 1875 farm house that has been restored as a museum depicting life in the mid-to-late 1800s. The house was built by Rochester merchant Timothy Whiting in what was then known as the city's "Lower Town" on North Broadway, just 3 1/2 blocks from its present location. The classic Victorian farm home was moved to Central Park in 1972.

Plummer Reflection

The Plummer Building, reflected in the windows of Wells Fargo Bank, was named in honor of Dr. Henry Plummer, who supervised its design and construction, and was one of the original partners of the Mayo brothers. In its early years, a flashing green and white beacon atop the tower guided aircraft into Rochester. The building has many ornate furnishings and is home to the historical suite, including the restored offices of Drs. Will and Charlie Mayo, and other historical pieces.

Pappageorge's

The Greek touch of the Pappas
family is evident in the décor of
Pappageorge Taverna, adjacent to
Michaels restaurant. Pappageorge is
the original family name before it
was shortened by Michael G. Pappas
when he immigrated from Greece.
Michaels is one of Rochester's oldest
and most popular restaurants, specializing in American and Greek dishes,
pastas and steaks. It was opened in
1951 by Michael Pappas' four sons.

Old Armory

The 1915 Armory is of the medieval fortress school of armory design. The site was purchased from Rochester Creamery Co. by the state on July 7, 1915. In August 1977, the Minnesota Army National Guard moved to its new headquarters on Marion Road. The Rochester City Council purchased the property that year for $45,000 and it is now home to the Rochester Senior Citizens Center. The building is on the National Register of Historic Places.

Fourth of July

The annual Fourth of July fireworks show has attracted thousands of people every year since the Post-Bulletin began sponsoring it in the 1950s. Many people crowd along the parkways and bike paths near Silver Lake, setting up lawn chairs during the day to get a prime viewing spot for the night-time show. Because the fireworks can be seen for miles, others choose to view from afar in their own back yards or neighborhood parks.

Old Library

Mayo Medical School's Mitchell Student Center began as the Rochester Public Library. Completed in 1937 by unemployed artisans working with the federal Work Projects Administration, the library cost $178,000. Mayo Foundation, which had donated the land for the building, purchased it in 1971 when the decision was made to establish Mayo Medical School. Major improvements were completed in 1985 to prepare to rename the building the Ruth and Frederick Mitchell Student Center.

FMC Razor Wire

The federal Bureau of Prisons purchased the former Rochester State Hospital campus for $14 million in 1984. The purchase was a divisive issue in the community, but since then, the Federal Medical Center has been a quiet neighbor. It opened in October 1984 with 19 inmates, and today holds about 800. The prison has housed various famous or notorious prisoners through the years, including the Rev. Jim Bakker, U.S. Rep. Dan Rostenkowski and political extremist Lyndon LaRouche.

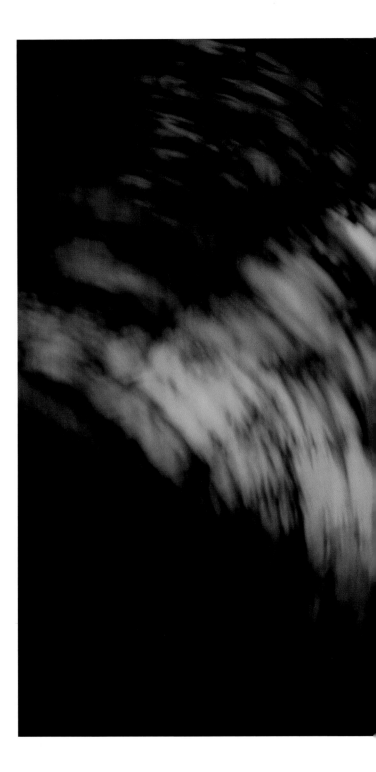

Riverfront Mural

"Rochester Riverfront Mural," created in 1994 by Winona artist Anne Scott Plummer, was part of Rochester's $105 million flood control project. The mural depicts the history and progress of the Rochester area with images that include an American Indian communal pipe, Conestoga wagons, bison, Canada geese, a computer, corn and the Plummer Building. The waterfall is discharge from the Franklin heating station which supplies heat to the Mayo Clinic.

Mayo Civic Center

A statue of the Mayo brothers greets visitors at the front of the Mayo Civic Center, a city-owned complex with an arena, exhibit halls and theaters that has been expanded over the years on the site of Mayo Park. The original building, called Mayo Civic Auditorium, was a gift from Dr. Charles H. Mayo and the Mayo Properties Association. The $450,000 building opened in 1939 with an ice revue by the St. Paul Skating Club. The statue was originally part of a 1952 memorial to the Mayos.

Dee Cabin

Built in 1862 on land where the Best Western Soldiers Field Tower & Suites now stands, the Dee cabin was constructed with poplar logs for about $ 25. The cabin's namesake, William Dee, was a shoemaker. Dee, his wife, Bridget, and their four children lived in the cabin for 15 years. After that, the cabin changed hands many times and was moved to several sites before coming to the Olmsted County History Center in 1987.

IBM

"Big Blue" opened its Rochester plant in 1958 in what was then a cornfield northwest of Rochester. It boosted the local economy with 1,750 jobs and by the late 1990s, the plant employed almost 5,000. After manufacturing more than 20 different business machines, the plant's focus shifted to the development and manufacture of the AS/400 computer models. Recognized for its efficiency and innovation, the Rochester plant won the 1990 Malcolm Baldrige National Quality Award.

Winter Flock

A giant Canada goose flaps a warning to its floating gaggle on Silver Lake. At times, the geese flee from humans, but many times visitors to the lake can get a close-up view by feeding dried corn to the geese, who quickly gather for the handouts. Silver Lake, home to the geese, is a manmade 25-acre lake that was formed in 1936 when a Work Projects Administration project dammed the south branch of the Zumbro River.

Downtown at Night

The Rochester Marriott sits at First
Avenue and First Street Southwest,
a corner that reflects the changes of
Rochester. A hotel has been on the
downtown corner ever since 1912.
The original was the Zumbro Hotel,
built by John H. Kahler. The hotel
established one of the very early
connections to Mayo Clinic buildings with a pedestrian bridge and a
pedestrian subway. Demolished in
1987, it was replaced by The Kahler
Plaza Hotel. It became the Rochester
Marriott in 1998.

Mayowood Lake

One of Dr. Charles H. Mayo's recre-
ational farming projects was raising
Canada geese. He started his flock
in the early 1920s with a pair from
either the Dakotas or Michigan. The
geese eventually strayed and dis-
persed locally, making their home
on Mayowood Lake and elsewhere
around Rochester. The lake, with its
series of island gardens, was created
when Dr. Charlie diverted the path of
the Zumbro River to create a dam to
produce electricity for Mayowood.

Silver Lake Bridge

Four Canada geese ascend over a
stone bridge that spans to an island at
Silver Lake in the southeast corner of
the park. Visitors to Silver Lake can
find geese on the lake and scamper-
ing around in the park at almost any
time of day, any time of year.
Thousands of the giant Canada geese
(branta Canadensis maxima) make
their home in Rochester, and the
city's seal includes the outstretched
wings of a goose.

Charlton Building

The Charlton Building, initially called Mayo North, is named after Ruth Charlton Mitchell Masson of Rochester and her family. Staff began moving into the $35 million building on the west side of Rochester Methodist Hospital in 1988. Five stories were added to the building in 2000, making it 10 stories. The building, which houses Mayo's Transplant Center as well as other medical departments, is connected to the Gonda Building on the south through a series of skyways and a pedestrian subway tunnel.

Gonda Atrium

The Gonda Building's flowing Nathan Landow Atrium floods the area with natural light on the building's east side. The 6,500-pound "Man and Freedom" statue hangs on the Mayo Building's north wall, which also serves as Gonda's south wall. The statue was commissioned for the Mayo Building in 1952. It was crafted by Croatian-born artist Ivan Mestrovic. The 28-foot sculpture was taken down during construction of the Gonda Building, allowing experts to inspect and clean it before returning it to the wall.

Cobblestone Street

Rochester paved its streets for the first time in 1905. This stretch of brick pavement still serves as the roadway for Ninth Avenue between Sixth and Seventh Streets Southwest in Rochester's "Pill Hill" neighborhood. It is the last street in the city that has maintained its brick surface. The bricks on many streets have been paved over with asphalt. First Avenue between Second and Fourth Streets Southwest was the city's first paved street.

Plummer House

The Plummer House, the former
home of Dr. Henry Plummer,
serves as a gathering and reception
place run by the Rochester Park &
Recreation Department. Captured
on a quiet snowy day, it is one of
the few times when the home and
its grounds are quiet. From spring
through fall, the grand home is busy
with receptions and gatherings, or
serving as the backdrop for wedding
and graduation photos.

W.W. Mayo Monument

Following the death of W.W. Mayo
in 1911, a citywide fund drive
solicited donations from individuals,
raising $5,000 to erect a bronze
memorial statue of "The Old
Doctor." Erected in Mayo Park in
1915, it was later moved to the west
side of the Mayo Civic Center complex. Soon it will stand in a new
park west of the Gonda Building,
along with a statue of Sister Mary
Alfred Moes.

Saint Marys Summit

The summit of the Francis Building's tower section at Saint Marys Hospital has housed a statue of Our Lady of the Holy Rosary since its construction in 1941. The lighted tower can be seen from many miles away. The Francis Building honors the Franciscan sisters who have served the hospital since its beginning in 1889. Five of the hospital buildings are named in honor of Saint Marys' foundress, Mother Alfred, and the administrators who followed her: Sisters Joseph, Domitilla, Mary Brigh and Generose.

Mayowood Mansion

Mayowood was the 3,000-acre country estate of Dr. and Mrs. Charles H. Mayo, southwest of Rochester on wooded land adjoining the Zumbro River. The estate included eight working farms. The home was visited by numerous notables of the day, including President Franklin D. Roosevelt, Helen Keller, Emperor Haile Selassie of Ethiopia, and the King and Queen of Nepal. In 1965, the house and 10 acres of surrounding land were donated to the Olmsted County Historical Society.

Stone Fence

The inspiration for Dr. Charles H. Mayo's stone fence came from his travels in the English and Scottish countryside. Mayowood's quarry provided the stones for the fence. Large triangular stones, pointed up at 2-foot intervals, top the fence. In the British Isles, the idea was to fence-in sheep, animals Dr. Charlie didn't raise. In the mid-1920s to 1930s, the fence ran nearly five miles toward town along Mayowood Road. Small sections of the wall remain today.

Rochester's History

Much of the recorded history of Rochester begins in 1854 when George Head laid claim to land along the Zumbro River. He spent that first summer carving out the spot from the long prairie grass along the meandering river and built his cabin on what is now South Broadway, just past Fourth Street Southwest.

Named after the city in New York where Head once lived, the settlers also chose "Broadway" for one of the first street names, reflecting their belief of the town's expected growth and greatness.

Broadway was first established as a main street when settlers hitched a large tree trunk to a team of oxen and dragged it sideways through the brush to mark the route.

Within a year, thousands of settlers began their push into Minnesota from other Midwestern states as well as the East Coast, especially New York. The region around Rochester is dotted with the names of New York cities.

Central School, pictured at right, towered as the city's tallest building after it was built in 1868. In 1910, a fire burned the top two floors and both towers of the school. Although it survived the fire, the school was torn down in 1950 to make way for the Mayo Building. *(Courtesy Olmsted County Historical Society)*

Today, the site of Head's first home is where thousands of cars and trucks course north and south on Broadway, a four-lane, paved roadway. The river is guided by concrete slabs and rocks placed there as part of a flood control project to keep the river within its banks.

Now, the city stretches for miles in every direction. Rochester covers the valley that Broadway follows and stretches far past the wooded hills that Head could see from his spot on the little river. Few could ever have guessed that from such a small beginning would grow to what is now Minnesota's third-largest city.

But who could have guessed it even when the U.S. Army's surgeon came to town in 1863, just a year after the U.S.-Dakota Indian war in the territory west of here? That's when Dr. William Worrall Mayo moved to Rochester from Le Sueur, Minn. His time with the Army was busy and filled with controversy. Despite that, he remained in the city after his service and began the medical practice that his sons later joined. Through references from train conductors and travelers, it soon was referred to as "Mayo's Clinic" and the name was eventually adopted.

The images in Dean Riggott's book capture the beauty of today's Rochester while showing the glimmers of the past that have blended into the community's scenery and architecture. Included in this book are pictures of Rochester's early years, courtesy of the Olmsted County Historical Society and Mayo Historical Unit, which offer visual depth to the written history about the city's growth.

Head's homestead site was a good one. Thirty-five years later, it was the approximate site of Rochester's Central Fire Station, a towering brick edifice with two balconies and a clock tower topped by a flag pole. The station was placed in the center of Broadway near Fourth Street Southwest to aid firefighters as they wrestled for control of the horse teams that bolted from the station's two bay doors, pulling the fire wagons north past the Cook Hotel.

In the late 1800s, Rochester developed into an agricultural center and mills and elevators sprouted up in the city. As a mark of its prominence in farming, Rochester hosted the Minnesota State Fair in 1866, 1867 and 1868, and then again for a three-year run from 1880 to 1882.

The grain from farmers filled the mills, but it also helped fuel Rochester's brewery, the Schuster Brewery. Opened as the Union Brewery in 1858, Henry Schuster bought the operation in 1866. The brewery building was lost to a fire in 1871, but when the company rebuilt, it increased its capacity. The brewery continued its success for several more decades before closing Jan. 1, 1922, a victim of Prohibition. Today, collectors scour the flea markets and antique stores looking for Schuster memorabilia.

As agriculture spread and the treaties with American Indians were enforced, the last Indians living in the area were said to have camped during the winter of 1865 near Rochester. The Dakota and some Winnebago were the original tribes of the region prior to the Treaty of Traverse des Sioux when the United States purchased much of the region west of Rochester from the tribes.

Missionaries and ministers were among the first immigrants and Rochester soon had fledgling churches. They initially struggled as many of the men were involved with the Civil War.

But the churches maintained their ties to the community and grew as the soldiers returned and the city continued growing. The Baptists were the first to build a church in Rochester, historians say. Their first formal service was conducted in October 1858 and they held baptismal services behind the church in the nearby Zumbro River. Calvary Episcopal Church is the oldest church building in Rochester. It stands at its original site at Second Street and Third Avenue Southwest on land donated by Head. The parish was established in 1860 and the church was consecrated in 1866. The stained-glass Tiffany & Co. windows have been maintained in the church throughout its history.

With the city taking shape, citizens elected Moses Fay, an attorney from New York and one of the town's early settlers, its first mayor. He served from 1858 to 1859.

Newspapers also began to publish to keep the young city's citizens informed. Among the first was the *Rochester Democrat*, which lasted only two years. But soon others, such as the *Rochester City News* and the *Rochester City Post*, came onto the scene. The *City Post*, which began publishing in 1859, was known as the Republican paper for its editorial stance and it found a receptive audience. In 1891, the *Rochester Daily Bulletin* appeared as the city's first daily newspaper. The *City Post* and the *Daily Bulletin* consolidated in 1925 into the *Rochester Post-Bulletin*, the newspaper that continues to serve the city today.

The beginning of the Mayo family's relationship with Rochester started when William Worrall Mayo arrived in 1863, but his path to Rochester was a circuitous one.

After immigrating from England, W.W. Mayo, who would father Dr. Will and Dr. Charlie Mayo, settled in Indiana in the 1840s, but was plagued by a recurrent illness (some think it was malaria, but no one knows for sure). He had a restless nature and set off in 1854, leaving his wife and children behind, to explore the new Minnesota Territory. He traveled by canoe and on foot between southern Minnesota and Duluth on several occasions, and was the original census taker and chairman of the county commission for St. Louis County (Duluth). He settled in Le Sueur with his family in 1858 until after the start of the Civil War and the Sioux Uprising in New Ulm, Minn., in 1862. He moved to Rochester in 1863 to be the regional examining surgeon for the Union Army. His territory included the southern half of the state. After the Civil War, he continued to practice medicine and to raise his young family in Rochester.

In the summer of 1883, two tornadoes changed the history of Rochester. On July 21, a tornado swept through Olmsted County, causing much damage. One month later, on Aug. 21, another tornado swept through the heart of Rochester about 7 p.m., destroying much of the small town, killing more than 30 people and injuring many more. Charlie and Dr. Will

Mayo were driving through town when the storm blew a cornice off the Cook Hotel and struck their buggy. They found shelter in a nearby blacksmith's shop.

The Sisters of the Order of St. Francis, lead by Mother Mary Alfred Moes, cared for many of the injured, as did Dr. W.W. Mayo and his two young sons – Will who had just received his medical degree, and Charlie who was only 18 years old and still five years away from his medical degree. Sister Alfred, having dedicated the Academy of Our Lady of Lourdes in Rochester in 1877, was inspired to start a hospital for the care of the sick and injured. Mother Alfred prevailed on Dr. W.W. Mayo to agree to be the medical director at the hospital. It took some convincing, but after assurances that the nuns would raise $40,000 and staff the hospital, Dr. Mayo agreed to the plan. The hospital was opened Oct. 1, 1889.

"The Old Doctor" as he was called, included his sons in the practice, and they assumed leadership of the hospital as he gradually retired. The hospital grew from 45 to 180 beds in its first 20 years of operation. The fame of the Mayos and the outpatient portion of their practice grew in the same period and beyond.

Horse-drawn carriages line the sides of South Broadway, which in 1889 was a dirt roadway. Several buildings from this north view at Fourth Street still stand today housing a law office, theater, retail stores, art galleries and a photo studio. *(Courtesy Olmsted County Historical Society)*

The growth of Saint Marys Hospital secured Rochester's place in the region as more than an agricultural center. With the renown that was beginning to grow with the Mayo brothers' skills and the demand for care that came with it, Rochester was starting to establish itself as a medical-based community.

The need for additional hospital space continued to grow. John H. Kahler, manager of the Cook Hotel, formed a company that built and staffed additional hospital space for Mayo Clinic. The first Kahler Hotel opened in 1907. It served as a convalescent hotel that included surgical facilities. The original Kahler was renamed the Damon Hotel after a larger Kahler Hotel, currently The Kahler Grand Hotel, opened in 1921. Kahler's Zumbro Hotel, which opened in 1912, had its own operating room. The new Kahler topped that with three operating rooms at the top of the hotel.

Eventually, the hotels converted solely to the business of serving guests' overnight needs and moved away from the hospital side of their business. Many of the city's early hotels are gone, but some, such as The Kahler continue to thrive.

Hospitals also blossomed. Kahler's corporation opened other downtown hospitals. Colonial Hospital opened in 1915 and expanded several times. It was acquired by Rochester Methodist Hospital in 1954 and a portion of the hospital building is still used by Mayo Clinic. Worrall Hospital was opened by Kahler four years after Colonial. At the site of today's Hilton and Guggenheim buildings, it was named in honor of the Mayo brothers' father. Curie Hospital, another Kahler project, opened in 1920 and focused on X-ray and radium treatments. It later housed a cafeteria that provided meals and dietary assistance to Mayo Clinic patients. The building was razed in 1963 when an annex to The Kahler Hotel was built.

Not all hospitals were demolished. Some moved. Today's Maxwell Guest House first started as the Rochester Hotel before it was converted by Kahler to the Olmsted Hospital, no relation to the current Olmsted Medical Center's operations. Kahler used the 65-bed space in 1921 to provide medical services for eight physicians. The physicians moved a year later to Saint Marys Hospital when a new surgical building opened. The Olmsted Hospital also provided space for Rochester Calorie Kitchen until it was moved to the Curie Hospital in 1926 and became the Rochester Diet Kitchen. Serving as a nurse's home, the building was moved in 1928 to a site on Second Avenue and Fifth Street Southwest. After Rochester Methodist Hospital dropped its separate nursing program, it became the Maxwell Guest House.

The need for additional hospital space continued to grow in Rochester in the early 1900s. John H. Kahler bought the E.A. Knowlton mansion at Second Avenue Southwest and West Center Street. The home was remodeled and added onto as it was converted into a hotel in 1907.

(Courtesy Olmsted County Historical Society)

Some of Rochester's old hotels still exist among the newer, modern hotels that keep Rochester's hospitality industry humming, serving Mayo Clinic patients as well as a thriving weekend convention and athletic competition business. Old hotels that still stand today include the Hotel Parker, now the Civic Inn on East Center Street; Hotel Martin, now the Colonial Inn downtown on Second Street Southwest; Hotel Francis, now the Candlerose Inn on Fourth Street Southwest; Hotel Carlton, now the Days Inn at West Center and First Avenue Northwest; and the Lawrence Hotel, the former Aldrich Nursery School near Silver Lake.

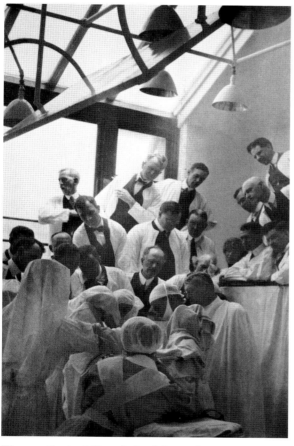

The medical skills of the Mayos began to garner attention from other physicians, who regularly visited to watch the surgical procedures practiced at the Rochester clinic. In 1892, the three Mayo physicians began to invite other physicians to join their growing medical practice. *(Photo: Mayo Clinic)*

It was Mayo Clinic's growth that fueled the rise in hotels and hospitals. In 1892, the three Mayo physicians began inviting partners to join their practice. They looked for physicians with specialties that could complement their practice and help it grow. It was the beginning of the group practice idea that has been further developed, refined and expanded at Mayo Clinic more than 100 years later. The Mayos added numerous staff members and within 23 years had six partners: Dr. Augustus W. Stinchfield in 1892; Dr. Christopher Graham in 1894; Drs. Melvin C. Millet and Henry S. Plummer in 1906; Dr. Edward Starr Judd in 1907; and Dr. Donald C. Balfour in 1915. Partners shared to a specific extent in the income but not in the ownership of the practice.

Dr. W.W. Mayo died in 1911 at the age of 91. Three years later, in 1914, on the site of the Mayo family's first home, the Mayo brothers had their own medical building constructed. The redbrick, five-story building at the site of today's Siebens Building was the first one designed specifically for the Mayo group practice and later became referred to as "The 1914 Building."

Dr. William Worrall Mayo poses with his sons, Dr. Charlie, left, and Dr. Will, right, around 1900. The elder Mayo took his sons to medical society meetings when they were young, exposing them to medicine long before they attended medical school. *(Courtesy Olmsted County Historical Society)*

More buildings would follow, but first the Mayo brothers were to establish the practice in a way that would maintain it for many decades to come.

In 1919, the Mayo brothers turned over their personal assets to form what eventually became Mayo Foundation, a charitable, not-for-profit corporation. The structure allowed for continued growth and planned for the Mayos' eventual retirement. The plan also made the entire medical staff salaried, so the focus would remain on the patient's needs.

Much was happening downtown. Around the time the first Mayo Building was built, Dr. Charlie proposed the start of a two-year university program. It would eventually become Rochester Junior College, what we today call Rochester Community and Technical College, Minnesota's oldest community college. At its start in 1915, 17 students were enrolled and were housed in classrooms at Rochester High School near downtown. It took more than 50 years for the school to transfer from the public school building to its own campus in southeast Rochester. In 1968, students and faculty moved into the new buildings. The campus has seen continued growth in its enrollment and facilities. Today the campus is called University Center Rochester and houses three main institutions: RCTC, University of Minnesota and Winona State University.

With growing reputations in the medical world, Drs. Charlie and Will built their own homes in 1911 and 1918, respectively. Dr. Charlie's Mayowood was a 3,000-acre estate that included stables, barns, a dairy and a greenhouse. Dr. Charlie's family lived in the home for more than 50 years until it and 10 acres were donated in 1965 to the Olmsted

County Historical Society. Dr. Will's home, now called Mayo Foundation House, was built at the then-edge of the city in southwest Rochester. The Tudor-style, Kasota stone exterior gave the mansion a stately appearance. Dr. Will had an office in the fourth floor tower where he was known to retire to read some of his favorite books: Westerns. The home was donated to Mayo Foundation in 1938 and is used for meetings and banquets.

Another prominent home is Dr. Henry Plummer's. Built on a southwest Rochester quarry, the home is known today as the Plummer House of the Arts. Dr. Plummer filled the home with many ingenuities. The 1924 house included an intercom, a central vacuum system and the first gas furnace in the city. His wife, Daisy, who lived long after Dr. Plummer's death in 1936, donated the home to the Rochester Park & Recreation Department. The home is used for meetings, receptions and special occasions.

As beautiful homes were going up in Rochester's neighborhoods, perhaps the most significant addition to the city's skyline was the Plummer Building, completed in 1928. At the time, it stood as the state's tallest building at 295 feet tall. The building's original plans did not include a carillon tower, but its distinctive four-story carillon tower was added during construction after Dr. William J. Mayo became fascinated with the bells during a trip to Belgium. The tower first held 23 bells that came from a foundry in England. The bells were a gift from Drs. Will and Charlie and were dedicated to the American soldier. Its height made it a perfect place for a beacon that sat atop the tower to guide aircraft into the city. In 1977, 33 additional bronze bells were added as a gift from descendants of Rochester pioneer Alphonso Gooding.

Residents lined the streets and sidewalks of Broadway to view the Rochester Automobile Dealers parade on March 24, 1927, as part of the Merchant's Spring Opening. The procession moved south on Broadway toward the Rochester Fire Department Central Station. *(Courtesy Olmsted County Historical Society)*

But as the Roaring '20s halted, the Great Depression of the 1930s slowed Rochester's economic boom. The tough times cut into the number of patients who visited Mayo Clinic. The rations and economic hardships required of citizens during World War II also limited visitors to Rochester, hurting the clinic and the supporting hospitality industry.

It was a difficult time for many reasons. Also during this time, the Mayo brothers scaled back their work and retired. Dr. Will retired in 1928 and a year and a half later, Dr. Charlie stepped down after a series of strokes greatly limited his surgical abilities. The brothers left Mayo Clinic's governing body in 1932 and died within two months of each other in 1939 – Dr. Charlie of pneumonia on May 26, and Dr. Will on July 28 in his sleep while he was recovering from surgery for stomach cancer. There was great mourning of the loss of the brothers. The Plummer Building's massive bronze doors were closed to mark each man's passing. The doors have only been closed a handful of times to mark the passing of significant members of Mayo Clinic or the nation, such as President Kennedy in 1963.

The Mayo brothers are buried together with their parents and their wives in their family plot in Rochester's Oakwood Cemetery. The epitaph on Dr. Charlie's headstone reads: "He lived abundantly" and Dr. Will's reads: "He loved the truth and sought to know it."

By the 1950s, growth was pervasive and there was great change on the horizon. Mayo Clinic officials turned the first shovel of dirt in 1950 preparing for its 12-story diagnostic building with special attention paid to systems that would promote efficient scheduling and routing of patients to the physicians and their examination rooms. The old Central School was torn down to make way for the Mayo Building which was completed in 1955. Another nine stories were added to the building in 1969.

A new hospital came on the scene in 1955. Olmsted Community Hospital opened its doors to patients. The 55-bed hospital was designed to serve the patients of non-Mayo Clinic physicians and received encouragement from many

In 1927, the Plummer Building nearly stood alone on the Rochester skyline. A revolving beacon atop the building guided airplanes into the city. The picture shows Second Street Southwest from Broadway, including the E.A. Knowlton Department Store and the Olmsted Bank & Trust building.
(Courtesy Olmsted County Historical Society)

in the community, including many affiliated with Mayo Clinic. Dr. William F. Braasch, a former Mayo Clinic urologist and the 12th member to join the Mayo Clinic staff, was a primary backer of the campaign to open the hospital.

In 1954, the Kahler hospital holdings and related properties were transferred to Methodist Hospital for approximately $3 million. The new organization became Rochester Methodist Hospital, however, a new hospital would not be built until 1966. It's known today as the Eisenberg Building.

Meanwhile, a new industry in Rochester was about to get its launch. Rochester boosters were euphoric when IBM President Thomas J. Watson Jr. announced in February 1956 that the city had been selected by the computer giant as the site of a new $8 million manu-facturing plant. Rochester's quality workforce and quality of life were recognized as sig-nificant assets. Carved from a cornfield, the IBM plant north of Rochester generated 1,750 new jobs immediately and has maintained a workforce that has numbered 5,000 or more for years. The company has expanded numerous times since its beginning and now has more than 2 million square feet of space.

And just as other industries grew in support of Mayo Clinic, companies grew from the presence of IBM. Pemstar, which is run by several former IBM employees, is an example of a company that has grown and expanded its business beyond that of IBM support. The computer industry also helped balance out the city's primary reliance on Mayo Clinic's fortunes. In coming to town, IBM brought many citizens who became leaders in civic and education organizations.

South of the IBM site in 1954, the Sisters of St. Francis were completing the construction of their home, Assisi Heights. The motherhouse, atop a hill in a rolling orchard, served as home for the sisters and is a prominent landmark today. The motherhouse resembles the Assisi, Italy, basilica and Franciscan convent.

Northwest Rochester was set for a growth pattern after IBM's arrival. Many of the homes and schools near Assisi Heights and IBM were constructed in the years that followed IBM's arrival. John Marshall High School opened for students in 1958, one month before IBM dedicated its new plant. Northwest Rochester continues to be a growth corridor for the city now stretching miles past the once lonely cornfield that IBM chose for its plant.

Heading into the 1960s, Rochester's airport was moved in 1961 from its site in southeast Rochester to its current site six miles south of the city to accommodate larger aircraft and encourage more flights.

As air travel continued to grow in popularity, the train traffic that first helped fuel Rochester's growth and was later used by Dr. W.W. Mayo to quickly reach a patient or transport one to better care, was drawing to a close. The "Rochester 400," so named because of the 400 miles in 400 minutes the trains could run, pulled out of the city's station for the last time with passengers on July 23, 1963, bound for Chicago. The *Rochester Post-Bulletin* said Theodore Hanson of La Crosse, Wis., a Mayo Clinic patient, was the last person to buy a ticket on the eastbound train. The city has not had regular passenger rail service since then.

Growth was reaching the city's schools as its major industries pulled in more employees. In 1966, a second public high school, Mayo High School, opened in southeast Rochester.

The growth of Mayo Clinic helped portions of downtown Rochester, but city officials were lobbying hard for an urban renewal project in 1969. It was a hotly contested issue and was defeated in a citywide election. Long-time Mayor Alex Smekta, a supporter of the plan, decided not to seek another term, but he returned to office in 1973 and served to 1979.

As debate raged about giving the downtown a makeover, the era of shopping centers arrived. Apache Mall opened in southwest Rochester in October 1969 and was soon to begin drawing stores and shoppers away from downtown to its indoor venue. Back in 1952, Miracle Mile had opened a strip mall on the city's west side.

The city's education offerings grew in the 1970s. Minnesota Bible College came to town, moving from its base in Minneapolis. Today, the school is called Crossroads College. In 1972, 40 students began classes in the new Mayo Medical School. The school was different than most medical schools of the era. It focused on small class sizes, close work between students and instructors, and experiences that would give students an early exposure to patient care. Today, it is one of the most competitive programs in the country.

The night of July 5, 1978, would change Rochester forever. A rain storm started in the early evening and by the morning of July 6, floodwaters raged down the Zumbro River and one of its tributaries, Bear Creek. The water rose to 11 feet above flood stage, soaking homes and businesses and forcing at least 5,000 residents from their homes. Rochester had experienced floods dating back to the early days of the settlers, but this one killed five people and wiped out an estimated $75 million in property, mainly on the city's southeast side.

In the flood's aftermath, the city joined with federal lawmakers to get a flood control project approved that would channel the river. After much debate, including an agreement to use some city sales tax money to aid the $105 million project, the plan to deepen the river channel and create pools to hold storm water moved ahead. Today, the river remains within its banks and miles of bicycle and walking trails were created next to the river's and creeks' routes.

The trails were new recreation opportunities in a city already graced with lush parks. Some of the parks came as gifts from the Mayo brothers and other benefactors. More parks have been added through the years as part of development plans for new neighborhoods in Rochester.

Dave Fritts of Rochester guides his boat south through the floodwaters on Third Avenue Southeast the morning of July 6, 1978. Fritts joined many Rochester residents in assisting flood victims. Although 5,000 people were evacuated, Fritts said many didn't want to leave their homes. *(Courtesy Olmsted County Historical Society)*

The city's next big debate didn't take long to surface. The Rochester State Hospital, which had been in operation since 1879, closed its doors in 1982. The buildings and grounds were sold to other government entities, and soon the federal government approached Olmsted County about the development of a federal medical prison. The debate was divisive. Nearby residents worried about security and the possible devaluation of their property. In the end, the Olmsted County Board voted to accept a $14 million bid from the federal Bureau of Prisons to purchase six buildings and 64 acres on the city's east side. Nineteen inmates were ushered into the facility in October 1984. Today, the facility houses more than 810 inmates. The prison has housed various famous or notorious prisoners through the years, including the Rev. Jim Bakker, U.S. Rep. Dan Rostenkowski and political extremist Lyndon LaRouche. The prison has been a good neighbor. Only one inmate has escaped in the prison's history, walking away from a work detail outside of the prison's razor wire in 1995. He was eventually captured more than a year later without incident in Iowa.

The mid-1980s brought continued change to Rochester. In 1986, Mayo Clinic joined with Rochester Methodist and Saint Marys hospitals to form one organization: Mayo Medical Center.

Downtown was busy. The Zumbro Hotel was demolished in 1987 to make way for a new hotel. Today, the property is the Rochester Marriott. Other structures went down as well, including the Masonic Temple, one of the early medical offices for the Mayos. The property became First Bank Centerplace. A year later and a block away on Broadway, the Radisson Hotel Centerplace was being built. The Centerplace Galleria shopping mall was also under construction, bringing a sweeping change to many of the downtown properties. Another block from the Galleria, Mayo Clinic dedicated the Siebens Building in 1989. It followed up the project with additions to its Hilton and Guggenheim buildings.

A perspective from the Plummer Building looking southwest sometime between 1950-55 shows, from the left along Second Street Southwest, the Congregational Church, nicknamed "The White Temple," the Wilson Club (formerly the Lawrence Hotel), a private residence, and the original First Presbyterian Church. *(Courtesy Olmsted County Historical Society)*

The changes in Rochester's downtown weren't the only ones. The faces of the city's citizens were also changing. An influx in the 1970s of Southeast Asian refugees brought the city new students, restaurants and stores. More immigrants would come as the 1980s gave way to the 1990s and more people were discovering Rochester as a good place to live.

Rochester's reputation was known regionally, but it gained nationwide attention in 1993 when *Money* magazine designated it as the best place to live in the United States based on rankings from its subscribers. Rochester Mayor Chuck Hazama gave a reporter for ABC's "20/20" a tour of the city from behind the wheel of a convertible. The news show aired nationally just prior to the release of the rankings. For many consecutive years after, Rochester ranked among the top cities in *Money's* rankings. The criteria and categories have changed for *Money's* rankings, but Rochester continues to find itself in the top tier of cities that are annually cited. Other "quality of life" surveys by magazines and consulting businesses regularly give credit to Rochester's overall quality of life.

Into the 1990s, Rochester saw an influx of immigrants from Ethiopia, Somalia, Sudan and Mexico. The promise of jobs, good medical care and a safe place to raise a family reached the ears of many and brought them here.

At times, the city has struggled with conflicts between longtime residents and the newcomers, but much of the initial strife fades as the newcomers adapt to their surroundings and residents become familiar with their new neighbors. Just as its early years, when immigrants were heard speaking German, Norwegian, Swedish and Gaelic, today Rochester remains a melting pot. There are more than 55 languages spoken by the students in Rochester's public schools.

As Rochester changes, it continues the image that George Head and other early settlers saw: this is a good place to live. Rochester has its own beauty and it's a place where people can live a good life and help others. Indeed, the journey to the Rochester of today has not always been smooth or without controversial times. But it's a city that continues to thrive and grow.

– Mike Dougherty is a freelance writer and editor. He is a graduate of the College of St. Thomas and is a former daily newspaper reporter. Mike lives in Rochester with his wife, Margaret, and their children, Jack, Katie and Martha. He also serves on the board of directors of Civic League Day Nursery, Rochester's oldest daycare center.

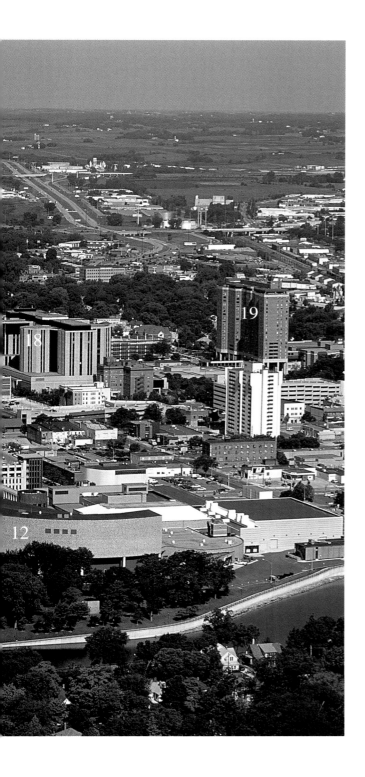

A Birds-Eye View

1. City Hall
2. Government Center
3. Historic Third Street
4. Vincent A. Stabile Building
5. Saint Marys Hospital
6. Guggenheim Building
7. Hilton Building
8. Mayo Building
9. Plummer Building
10. Centerplace Building
11. Zumbro River
12. Mayo Civic Center
13. Public Library
14. Peace Plaza/Galleria Mall
15. The Kahler Grand Hotel
16. Siebens Building
17. Gonda Building
18. Methodist Hospital
19. Charter House

Historical Facts & Figures:

1854 ~ Pioneers George Head and Thomas Simpson stake their claims along the Zumbro River. A settlement grows from these first homes and is named "Rochester" after Head's hometown of Rochester, N.Y.

1855 ~ Thomas Hunter surveys the original plat of the town of Rochester. The U.S. government sells land for $1.25 per acre.

1855 ~ Rochester's first post office opens in a log cabin near Cascade Creek.

1857 ~ Rochester is selected as the Olmsted County seat. The initial tally favored Marion, but in a recount, the discovery of voter fraud threw the decision to Rochester.

1862-65 ~ More than 1,200 Olmsted County men – a tenth of the population – enlist to aid the Union Army in the Civil War.

1863 ~ Dr. William Worrall Mayo is named examining surgeon for the 1st Military Enrollment Board (Civil War) by President Lincoln. Rochester is the headquarters of the board. Dr. Mayo arrives with his young family.

1864 ~ A passenger train car makes its first stop in Rochester on Oct. 8.

1865 ~ Charles Horace Mayo is born in Rochester on July 19. His brother, William James Mayo, was born in 1861 when the family lived in LeSueur, Minn.

1865 ~ Rochester Seminary opens and is the first school in the city to offer high school courses.

1866 ~ Calvary Episcopal Church is completed and consecrated on Jan. 28.

1868 ~ Central School opens with 14 rooms, becoming the tallest building in the city. The current Mayo Building sits on this site.

1870 ~ The Rochester Fire Department purchases its first fire engine. The engine, nicknamed "Little Giant," cost $9,500.

1877 ~ A new community of Sisters of Saint Francis of Our Lady of Lourdes forms under Mother Mary Alfred Moes in Rochester.

1879 ~ The second Minnesota Hospital for the Insane at Rochester opens.

1879 ~ Tradition suggests that at age 14, with only the use of pictures and descriptions he had seen, Charlie Mayo puts together the first telephone link in Rochester, connecting the office of his father, W.W. Mayo, to his farm residence in southeast Rochester.

1883 ~ After graduation from medical school in June, Dr. William J. Mayo joins his father in practice in the Ramsey Building. For 17 years, the Mayo partnership grew and flourished at this location before moving to the Masonic Temple in 1900.

1883 ~ On Aug. 21, a tornado (then called a cyclone) devastates the city, leaving 30 dead and hundreds injured and homeless. The Sisters of Saint Francis help local physicians care for the injured. Shortly after the tragedy, the nuns raise funds and convince Dr. W.W. Mayo to establish a hospital.

1888 ~ Charles Horace Mayo receives his medical degree from Northwestern University.

1889 ~ Saint Marys Hospital is established. With 27 beds, it becomes the first general hospital in southeastern Minnesota.

1889 ~ On Sept. 30, Dr. Charles H. Mayo performs the first surgical procedure at Saint Marys Hospital. The operating table is made of wood and built by Dr. Charlie.

1891 ~ On June 22, the *Rochester Daily Bulletin* publishes the city's first daily news-paper.

1892 ~ The three Mayo physicians begin to invite other physicians to join their growing medical practice. Each doctor has a specialty, so they combine their skills for the benefit of each patient. This principal of "group practice" remains the hallmark of Mayo today.

1894 ~ On March 15, the Municipal Light Plant is completed. Electricity is supplied from early evening to midnight to the business district and nearby homes.

1898 ~ The Rochester Public Library opens at First Avenue and Second Street Southwest. It is torn down in 1948.

1900 ~ On Nov. 29, the Mayo firm relocates to the new Masonic Temple building because the family practice has outgrown its offices in the Ramsey Building.

1906 ~ Saint Marys School of Nursing is organized, opening with two students.

1907 ~ The first hotel-hospital convalescent facility in the downtown area, The Kahler Hotel, hosts an open house for the general public.

1910 ~ Fire destroys the top floors and bell tower of Central School.

1911 ~ On March 6, Dr. William Worrall Mayo, 91, dies, just one month after he and his wife, Louise, celebrate their 60th wedding anniversary.

1911 ~ Amelia Witherstine is the first woman elected as a member of Rochester Board of Education. She is also the first woman to serve on an Olmsted County jury.

1912 ~ Construction of Mayowood (home of Dr. Charlie and Edith Mayo) is completed southwest of Rochester.

1912 ~ Heffron High School for boys and St. John's for girls are established. The schools later merge into the forerunner of today's Lourdes High School.

1912 ~ The Zumbro Hotel opens on the site of today's Rochester Marriott. It is the tallest building in the city. Immediately, 48 of the 122 beds are used by the Mayo practice for hospital patients.

1914 ~ The first Mayo Clinic is built at First Street and Second Avenue Southwest, formerly the site of the Mayo family home and today, site of Mayo's Siebens Building.

1915 ~ Rochester Commercial Club is organized by business and professional leaders to meet the needs of the growing city. It later becomes the Chamber of Commerce.

1915 ~ On Sept. 14, Minnesota's first public two-year college opens on the third floor of the Coffman Building.

1916 ~ The fortress style "Armory Hall" is completed and the building is dedicated on Feb. 3. Once the city's armory, it is now the home of the Senior Citizens Center.

1918 ~ Rochester City Council votes on July 9 to change the city's street names to numerical streets and avenues, replacing many of the names given to the roadways by Rochester's early settlers.

1918 ~ Dr. William J. Mayo builds a Tudor-style house with a Kasota stone exterior along Fourth Street Southwest. Today, the house is known as the Mayo Foundation House.

1919 ~ Dr. Will and Dr. Charlie turn over $2.5 million from their personal assets to form what is now Mayo Foundation, a charitable, not-for-profit corporation. The entire medical staff becomes salaried.

1921 ~ The present Kahler Hotel opens on Sept. 27.

1924 ~ Dr. Henry Plummer's 49-room English Tudor mansion is completed on a hill in southwest Rochester. It is now known as Plummer House of the Arts.

1925 ~ The Olmsted County Historical Society organizes.

1927 ~ On May 8, a nine-hole public golf course opens at Soldiers Field.

1927 ~ The Plummer Building is dedicated in June. It opens in 1928 and is Minnesota's tallest building, until Foshay Tower in Minneapolis opens the following year.

1927 ~ The formal opening of the Chateau Dodge Theatre takes place on Oct. 26.

1928 ~ Rochester Airways opens in west Rochester as the city's first organized airfield. Just one year later, it moves because of swampy soil conditions. Its new site in southeast Rochester is now the sites of Meadow Park and Mayo High School.

1929 ~ U.S. Secretary of State Frank B. Kellogg, a former Rochester attorney and U.S. senator, is awarded the Nobel Peace Prize for his promotion of the Briand-Kellogg Pact of 1928, which condemned war as a way to solve international controversies.

1929 ~ Reid, Murdock & Co. canning factory, now Seneca Foods, opens on June 18. It includes a water tower designed like an ear of corn to attract attention to the site.

1930 ~ On Jan. 7, Rochester citizens vote in support of a bond issue to build a new fire station. Plans call for the demolition of the fire station at the south end of Broadway and permit the state to extend Broadway south across the Zumbro River.

1930s ~ Silver Lake is developed as a Works Progress Administration (WPA) project as crews dredge the lake bed and dam the river at Broadway.

1934 ~ In a ceremony at Soldiers Field on Aug. 8, President Franklin Delano Roosevelt presents the Mayo brothers with the national American Legion award "for their distinguished services to mankind."

1936 ~ Rochester's first municipal swimming pool opens at Soldiers Field.

1939 ~ Mayo Civic Auditorium is donated to the people of Rochester by Dr. Charles H. Mayo and the Mayo Properties Association.

1939 ~ Dr. Charlie dies on May 26. Dr. Will dies on July 28.

1939 ~ Sister Mary Joseph Dempsey dies the same year as the Mayo brothers, compounding the loss to the Mayo and Saint Marys community. She was Dr. William J. Mayo's first surgical assistant and opened the Saint Marys Hospital School for Nurses.

1940 ~ Lobb Field (then Rochester Airport) is dedicated on Aug. 4 to mark the upgrades in facilities and runways at the airport. The field was named for A.J. Lobb, legal counsel and member of the administration at Mayo Clinic.

1946 ~ Rochester Art Center is incorporated on Nov. 15.

1948 ~ Silver Lake Municipal Power Plant begins operation. Using water from Silver Lake to cool the steam turbine, the warm water is routed back into the lake. Geese discover the ice-free water and gradually begin to winter on the lake.

1950 ~ Approximately 1,167 area men and women join the armed forces during the Korean War. Twenty-two are killed in action between June 25, 1950, and July 27, 1953.

1950 ~ On Aug. 18, the original Central School building is torn down to make way for construction of the Mayo Building.

1950 ~ On Dec. 10, Drs. Edward C. Kendall and Philip S. Hench of Mayo Clinic are awarded the Nobel Prize in Physiology or Medicine. They share in the award for the isolation and first clinical use of cortisone on April 13, 1949. Drs. Kendall and Hench are honored at a presentation in Stockholm.

1950s ~ Rochester is one of the first cities in the country with cable TV.

1951 ~ Rochester Civic Theater is founded.

1952 ~ Miracle Mile Shopping Center opens its stores on Oct. 8.

1954 ~ Assisi Heights opens its motherhouse for the Sisters of the Order of Saint Francis.

1955 ~ Olmsted Community Hospital opens on June 26. It is the first publicly owned hospital in the county. It is now called Olmsted Medical Center.

1955 ~ The Mayo Building is completed. Twelve stories are built at this time.

1956 ~ IBM announces plans to locate its sixth major plant in the United States at a site northwest of Rochester.

1958 ~ John Marshall High School opens in northwest Rochester on Sept. 2.

1961 ~ Rochester Municipal Airport moves to its current location south of Rochester.

1962 ~ Rochester Auto Park, the city's first parking ramp, opens at 14 Second St. S.E.

1962 ~ Wildlife experts identify the geese at Silver Lake as being Branta canadensis maxima, or giant Canada geese, a subspecies that biologists had considered extinct.

1963 ~ On July 23, the last passenger train to leave Rochester, "The Rochester 400," departs for Chicago on The Chicago and North Western Railroad.

1965-1975 ~ Twenty-four Olmsted County residents, serving as military personnel, are killed in the Vietnam War.

1966 ~ Rochester Methodist Hospital opens what is now known as the Eisenberg Bldg.

1966 ~ Mayo High School opens with a dedication ceremony on Aug. 31.

1968 ~ Luis W. Alvarez (Rochester High School class of 1928) is awarded Nobel Prize in Physics.

1969 ~ Apache Mall shopping center opens on Oct. 16.

1969 ~ The Mayo Building adds nine more floors to grow to 21 stories tall.

1970 ~ Harry A. Blackmun, former Mayo Clinic legal counsel, is appointed to the U.S. Supreme Court by President Nixon.

1971 ~ Minnesota Bible College moves from Minneapolis to Rochester.

1972 ~ Forty students enter Mayo Medical School.

1975 ~ Nancy Brataas, a Rochester Republican, is the first woman elected to the Minnesota Senate.

1978 ~ On July 6, floodwaters rise 11 feet above flood stage during the worst flood in the city's history. Five people die, an estimated 5,000 residents are evacuated and $75 million in property damage is recorded.

1981 ~ The first heart transplant at Saint Marys is performed on Feb. 8.

1982 ~ The Rochester State Hospital is closed, ending 103 years of existence. The property and buildings are sold to other government agencies.

1984 ~ On Oct. 8, the Mayo One medical helicopter begins its first day of service.

1984 ~ The Federal Medical Center opens in October with 19 inmates at the site of the former Rochester State Hospital.

1986 ~ Mayo Clinic merges with Saint Marys Hospital and Rochester Methodist Hospital to form Mayo Medical Center.

1987 ~ The Zumbro Hotel is demolished and The Kahler Plaza Hotel, later to become the Rochester Marriott, is erected in its place.

1987 ~ In June, the wrecking ball begins knocking down the Masonic Temple Building, the second office building of the Mayo family. It gives way to the First Bank Building Centerplace.

1988 ~ Originally called Mayo North, the superstructure of the Charlton Building, located to the west of Methodist Hospital, is completed in June.

1989 ~ The Centerplace Galleria mall opens to shoppers in May.

1989 ~ Mayo Clinic dedicates the Harold W. Siebens Medical Education Building on the site of W.W. Mayo's home and the 1914 Mayo Building.

1990 ~ Mayo Clinic's Hilton Building adds five floors of occupied space and one floor for mechanical equipment. The Guggenheim Building adds floors 12 through 21.

1993 ~ The $24 million Government Center is completed and opened to the public.

1993 ~ Higher education officials representing the Rochester Community and Technical College, Winona State University and the University of Minnesota join others to celebrate the formal opening of the $17 million, three-story brick University Center Rochester building that houses all three institutions.

1995 ~ The Rochester flood-control project is officially dedicated in September at a ceremony outside Mayo Civic Center. The $105 million project took eight years to complete.

1996 ~ Rochester loses one of its most visible promoters and ambassadors when Chuck Hazama retires after 16 1/2 years as the city's mayor.

1996 ~ Employees move into the new City Hall building connected to the Government Center, which houses Olmsted County government services.

1998 ~ Century High School is completed and dedicated in October.

1999 ~ *Money* magazine places Rochester among the top three most livable cities in the country for the seventh year in a row.

2000 ~ Dedication of Soldiers Field Veterans Memorial takes place on June 25.

2001 ~ Riverside Central becomes the first new public elementary school to open in three decades. It opens near the confluence of Bear Creek and the Zumbro River.

2001 ~ The Leslie and Susan Gonda Building is opened in October, adding more than 1.5 million square feet to the downtown Mayo Clinic campus. Total cost: $375 million.

2002 ~ A ground-breaking ceremony on Sept. 9 marked the start of construction for Rochester's tallest building, the 27-story, $60 million Broadway Plaza, which will include apartments and retail space at South Broadway and First Street Southeast.

2002 ~ Ground is broken on Nov. 12 for the new $6 million Rochester Art Center on the Mayo Civic Center's south side.

2003 ~ Construction begins on the expansion of 11 miles of U.S. 52. The $232 million project is the state's largest-ever single-bid highway project. Officials expect to finish by the end of 2006.

2004 ~ Rochester celebrates its sesquicentennial (150-year anniversary) with a slate of events through the year.

Interesting Mayo Facts:

Dr. William J. Mayo was a boxing champion at medical school. He was also told by a professor that he'd never succeed as a doctor.

Dr. Charles H. Mayo built the first operating room table for Saint Marys Hospital.

As physicians came to Rochester to see the Mayos operate, they frequently spoke of "the Mayo Brothers' Clinic" or "Mayo's Clinic" as their destination. The railroads and patients soon popularized this name, and in 1914 it was adopted as the clinic's name.

"Saint Marys" does not use an apostrophe because it shows possession and the sisters did not want it to appear that an individual or group owned the hospital.

Dr. William Worrall Mayo died from complications of a farm accident that occurred a year earlier when his left hand and forearm were crushed. Three operations were necessary and the last resulted in amputation of the injured hand and forearm. His health failed rapidly and he died on March 6, 1911. He was 91 years old.

The distinctive bell tower atop the Plummer Building was not part of the original design. It was added after Dr. Will became fascinated with carillons while on a medical trip to Belgium. At the time of construction, it was the tallest building in Minnesota.

Mayo Clinic occupies more than 13 million square feet of space in about 40 buildings, making it more than 2 1/2 times the size of the Mall of America.

In a typical year, about 315,000 patients register at Mayo Clinic, which translates into 1.21 million patient visits (individual visits with physicians) annually.

Mayo Clinic has 1,544 staff physicians and scientists and 2,451 residents, fellows, pre-doctoral and other students; total staff is more than 26,000, including 22,214 allied health staff.

Together, Saint Marys and Rochester Methodist hospitals provide more than 1,950 beds and 99 operating rooms.

The combined total of surgical cases performed each year is about 48,000.

Mayo Health System now includes clinics and hospitals in more than 60 communities in southern Minnesota, western Wisconsin and northern Iowa.

Photo Index:

The following sources were consulted in preparation of the foreword, history, captions, "Historical Facts & Figures" and "Interesting Mayo Facts" pages: Olmsted County Historical Society; Mayo Clinic Historical Unit; Rochester Post-Bulletin Co.; *Rochester: City of the Prairie* (Harriet W. Hodgson, 1989); *Mayo Roots* (Clark W. Nelson, 1990); *The Geese of Silver Lake* (Craig Blacklock, 1989); *The Unique Voice of Service: The Story of the Kahler Corporation, Rochester, Minnesota* (Clark J. Pahlas, 1964); *Dedicated to Excellence: The Rochester Methodist Hospital Story* (William Holmes, 1984); *Highlights of the Olmsted County Fair, 1860-1990* (Ray Aune, 1991); *Rochester: Mecca for Millions* (Harold Severson, 1979); *The Rochester Story* (Mearl W. Raygor, 1976); *History and Souvenir of Rochester* (Mrs. J.R. Willis, 1924); *The Rochester Centennial, 1854-1954* (Rochester Centennial Association, Inc., 1954); *Rochester Sketchbook* (Val Webb, 1976); *History of Olmsted County Minnesota* (Hon. Joseph A. Leonard, 1910); *The Doctors Mayo* (Helen B. Clapsattle, 1941); *Mayo Clinic: Its Growth and Progress* (Victor Johnson, 1984); *History of the Rochester Fire Department 1866-2000* (Minard Petersen, Betty and Elmer LaBrash, 2000); Ardell F. Brede; Cynthia Daube; Patrick Dean; Hoyt Finnamore; Charles Gagnon; John Hunziker; Christine Jensen; Ken & Joyce Kappauf; Kevin Kelly; John Kruesel; Gary Neumann; Charles Pappas; Dr. Paul Scanlon; Denny Stutz; Roy Sutherland; Dave Weber; Mark Weimer; Joanne Weygand; Allen Whipple; John Withers.

Special thanks to the following businesses and organizations for their help and cooperation: Assisi Heights, Aquarius Nightclub, Barnes & Noble Bookstores, Chardonnay Restaurant, Creative Cuisine Co., Daube's, The Federal Medical Center, IBM, John Kruesel's, Lanmark Inc., Mayo Foundation, Michaels Restaurant, Olmsted County Historical Society, Seneca Foods, Wells Fargo.

About the Author:

Rochester native Dean Riggott has worked as a professional photographer since 1991 when he began his career as a photojournalist for the *Post-Bulletin, Successful Business* and *Agri News* newspapers in Rochester.

Dean left his newspaper job in 1999 to devote full attention to his freelance business, Dean Riggott Photography, specializing in Rochester and agriculture photo stock, commercial, corporate, editorial and weddings. In 1997, Dean published his best-selling book, *Rochester: The Images,* and in 2001 he published *Life on the Farm: A Pictorial Journey of Minnesota's Farmland and its People.*

Dean's clients include, among others, Wells Fargo, Mayo Clinic, *Sierra Magazine, The Wall Street Journal, The New York Times, Successful Farming, Women's Health, Ladies Home Journal, Young Entrepreneur, International Investor,* Associated Press, and Bloomberg News. He is also a member of Grant Heilman Photography, the largest agricultural stock agency in the country.